I Open Fire

I Open Fire

Poems

David Pol

dead letter office

BABEL Working Group

punctum books * brooklyn, ny

I Open Fire: Poems
© David Pol, 2014.

http://creativecommons.org/licenses/by-nc-nd/3.0/

This work is Open Access, which means that you are free to copy, distribute, display, and perform the work as long as you clearly attribute the work to the authors, that you do not use this work for commercial gain in any form whatsoever, and that you in no way alter, transform, or build upon the work outside of its normal use in academic scholarship without express permission of the author and the publisher of this volume. For any reuse or distribution, you must make clear to others the license terms of this work.

First published in 2014 by
dead letter office, BABEL Working Group
an imprint of punctum books
Brooklyn, New York
http://punctumbooks.com

The BABEL Working Group is a collective and desiring-assemblage of scholar-gypsies with no leaders or followers, no top and no bottom, and only a middle. BABEL roams and stalks the ruins of the post-historical university as a multiplicity, a pack, looking for other roaming packs with which to cohabit and build temporary shelters for intellectual vagabonds. We also take in strays.

ISBN-13: 978-0692298268
ISBN-10: 0692298266

Cover Image: Jason Ponce, *Theater of Nation*, 2014.

***

Don't think too hard out loud.
If you open your mouth
I'll open fire.

I Open Fire

AUTOMATIC WEAPON

I showed you
how to work
the return mechanism
on an automatic weapon.

Your eyes within target range.
My adrenaline.

We detonate the night.

We set off the demolition
of our laundry.

I yell to you
through a mute.

I Open Fire

BLANKS

I chat with
an arms dealer.

He wears the green
tea of uniform.

He offers gunpowder treats
and shows me a garden
where ammo blooms.

He speaks in the
sharp rounds of a crow.

I respond
in blanks.

I OPEN FIRE

Hand

My inept hand
clammy with fear
fumbles with these cocked
words.

I aim for
our punctual hearts
which I destroy
with a direct hit.

I OPEN FIRE

A Night Without You

The sheets of the sky rip at the seams.
Lightning bolts wrestle. Tearing. Tossing.

Inside my body there are pieces of metal.
Nails.

The moon wears a ski mask.

I parachute downward.
A small black balloon
into a red forest.

I OPEN FIRE

SHELLS OF WORDS

Do you hear
what I'm shooting at you?

From the tree
fall the bodies of leaves.

From our mouths
which are boiling
fall the shells of words.

I OPEN FIRE

TAXI

We get into a taxi.
We drive into a cloud of dust.
Chances are we'll never drive out.

A mined bridge
runs toward us.

Birds fire into the sky.

I OPEN FIRE

Sapper

I dispose you precisely
delicately and cautiously.

Time ticks inside us.
Counting down.

And when the night goes off
the shock wave
throws us apart
toward each other.

I OPEN FIRE

MACHINE GUN

What sense is there in this life
that scurries away like a lizard?

My bayonet cuts the night
which is user friendly
like a machine gun.

I OPEN FIRE

SHOOTING RANGE

I take a look around the shooting range
as if playing with fire
will cure me.

On the city's temple
the scar of sunset.
Blood.

The air exhales
controlled substances.

My hand reaches
for the cool pistol.

Clouds gather.
Fear picks up
like wind.

I OPEN FIRE

WAR

War dreams lazily in the thicket.
The purring cellos of dissonant blades of grass.
A defused sky. Lightning like a night light.
Thunder from a distance.

We hope it will avoid our town.
We go for a beer at the local bar.
Someone runs after the moon
which someone threw in the river.
Almost nothing is happening.

We eat love. Spitting out the pits.
There's scrap metal in the cemetery.
They died, more or less. But nothing more.

I Open Fire

PROMETHEUS

My name is Prometheus.
I'm a celebrity.

I work in television
selling fire.

Zeus
my former enemy
edits a tabloid.

Sometimes we get
a time cramp
but it's already
past its expiration date.

1 OPEN FIRE

Deserter

I'm a deserter.
I'm walking with a pistol case
against traffic. Towards you.
Towards our love
which waits in the wings of hope
to play Distraction Herself.

I OPEN FIRE

WEDDING

An airplane
a multirole combat craft
has gotten tangled up
in your wedding dress.

In a veil of clouds
we fly, oversized.

I hold you in the arms
of arms.
Air. Earth.

We tell each other: I do.
We go off radar.

I OPEN FIRE

WHEN I TOUCH YOU

When I touch you
I think
we must be grappling.

I Open Fire

ZOMBIE

I am deathpositive.
Aimless. Sleepless.

I am
a remote controlled
zombie.

Above me
a supersonic
unmanned God.

Filled to the brim with you
I tear myself to bits.

I OPEN FIRE

LIFE

I execute my life
by firing squad.

And when my life
falls to the ground
I run to it calling out
that it was just a joke.

But my life is dead.

I don't know
how to live with that.

I OPEN FIRE

TEAR GAS

In your arms
I am an assassin suicide.

We explode always at the same moment
when you peel a wormy apple
and from my eyes
tear gas.

I Open Fire

My World

My world is critically injured.
It was ambushed.

An exploding mine
has ripped out its mind.

I carry it on a stretcher.
Its eyes are wide open
and it's screaming.

We are walking through
a boiling pressure cooker.

When the world dies
I dissolve
into the vapor.

I OPEN FIRE

God

God has gone missing,
the sniper.

He didn't notice
himself sliding hellward.

The rest
a torch.

David Pol was born on December 31, 1990. "Presently absent," as he describes himself, he is part of an elite secret service unit. He lives in Hell and *I Open Fire* is his literary debut.

W. dreams, like Phaedrus, of an army of thinker-friends, thinker-lovers. He dreams of a thought-army, a thought-pack, which would storm the philosophical Houses of Parliament. He dreams of Tartars from the philosophical steppes, of thought-barbarians, thought-outsiders. What distance would shine in their eyes!

~Lars Iyer

www.babelworkinggroup.org

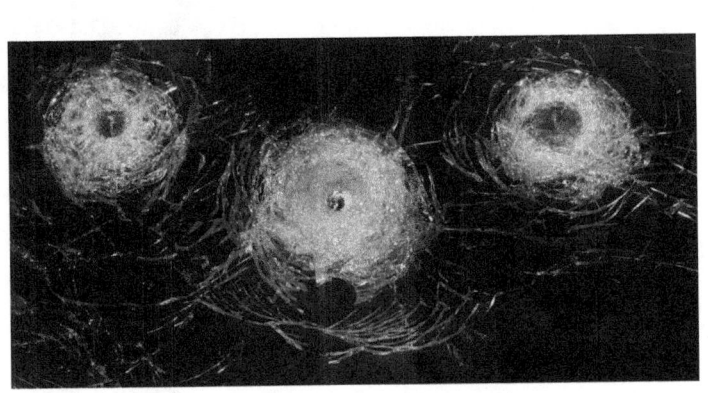

www.ingramcontent.com/pod-product-compliance
Lightning Source LLC
Chambersburg PA
CBHW070850160426
43192CB00012B/2383